CH091381549

lung iron

daniel fraser

ignitionpress

for Juno

First published in 2020
by **ignition**press
Oxford Brookes Poetry Centre
Oxford Brookes University
OX3 0BP

© Daniel Fraser 2020

*Daniel Fraser has asserted his right to be identified as author of this work
in accordance with the Copyright, Designs & Patents Act 1988.*

*This book is sold subject to the condition that it shall not, by way of trade or otherwise,
be lent, resold, hired out or otherwise circulated without the publisher's prior consent
in any form of binding or cover other than that in which it is published and without a
similar condition including this condition being imposed on the subsequent purchaser.*

Cover design: Flora Hands, Carline Creative

A CIP record for this book is available from the British Library

ISBN 978-1-9161328-6-3

Contents

Saoirse	1
Gospel Oak to Barking	2
Ants	4
Nocturnal Toolbox	6
Covenant	7
Change of Knowledge	8
Winter Window	10
Family Holiday	11
An Imagined Visit to the Pencil Museum	12
Haw	14
Familiar Road	15
Apophatic	17
Robert Mitchum	18
First Anniversary	19
Duration	21
Getting Over It	22
Shell	23
Hebden Bridge	24

*The troubled throng
Of words break out like smothered
   fire through dense
And smouldered wrong.*

Isaac Rosenberg, *Expression*

Saoirse

A shirtless man with a black mohawk is raking
dry leaves across the road

her name tattooed on his spine, letters a foot high,
blue Dunhill lip-hung and peeling

the uncaring lilt of decades pulling at that
sweet smoke, the pleasure of destruction transfigured

over muscle. Your back creaks like a knife
discoloured in the body of a whale

a beaching of something ancient
on a cold Atlantic shore, the carving

of sorrow into sustenance. I want to know
what broken bond, what gasp of newborn breath

could inaugurate this ink? Instead our mouths lay
soft as straw across the threshold of a speech left

quietly alone, eyes sharing a look that says
promises, that says *we are the rough bodies*

that know these afternoons, the blunt keepers
of words thickened into sinew. I say thank you

to the rays that burned us into being
and to her, the great shadow, gathered up

into this testament of skin.

Gospel Oak to Barking

Is there a line more suited to the disenchantment of the world?
The rumble of Truth's winged oaks, torn mad

by the braying dogs of modernity. Weber
reconfigured by logistics, tracked and signed west

to east: progress that follows its own lie
into the clipped lawns of a suburban sunrise.

Don't get mythic, the man in the lemon polo
implies, reading his tattoo out loud: *dream*

*as if you'll live forever, live as if you'll die
today* wrapped blue around a rose

his tasselled moccasins catching drips from
bags swollen with the goods of an anonymous grocer,

headphones and flower print leaking music
electronica somehow both angular and soft,

the tongue-shape of ochre or trigonometry
performed in crayon. Our exit reached we descend

from the Overground into the fragile tumult,
Janus-footed Harringey trundles along, stuck somewhere

between second and third, like Virgil, only licensed
to stand at the edges of the sky.

On Green Lanes MacDonald's and Argos vie for
lumens and the mattress store's neon *Dreams*

offer nothing but a place to rest. A man in
a three-piece sequin suit, hair brocaded with shells,

buys a knock-off Disney princess made of Victoria
sponge, her arms pierced by candles:

a wounded Ariel deflated as Sebastian.
The pavement kicks with warped fruit, kebab meat, and promises

of hot nuts. A Kurdish anarchist plays
the accordion, doling out film scores for the hair-netted cooks

folding shop-front dough: cheese, lamb, and spinach
parcelled into grease-paper, scent leaching

onto the poorly-councilled road, tar spots
clumped and chewy, the soft darkness walking with us

along the park where a row of poplars
turns untendered silver on the breeze. On our street

sparrows and starlings bathe their wings in the gutter,
flitting back to nests cloaked above estate agents

and franchised coffee: harbingers of high rent and
dislocation. By the corner a woman hands

out papers for her new congregation, the name
on the leaflet is Madame Zendah: *hear the words*

of Christ £3, tea leaves read just £5 a cup,
enquiries regarding salvation also permitted.

Ants

Consider the ways we hunt for dereliction;
young bodies coppery, objectless urges, hands

fraught with ruin, taut with lust. Our playground
a dank railway meadow of buttercups
and daisies, puddles trudged
with gravel and cement
where discarded sofas exhibit exposed foam

and monoxide poppies, mean and anaemic, sway
in the September heat.

They come without calling,
a kind of returned earth;

lines of beads shivering straight;
tarry droplets, marching night.

Their thousand jaws clenched like
hands frozen into prayer;

a dark parade of certainty
patterned into chaos.

On merciless afternoons we broke them;
spry limbed, raw as nettles. Eleven and
twelve: those low ages incapable of guilt
       our feet drumming,
kicking out catastrophes
          like gods cancelling crops of blackened grain.

Again they came, lines warped below our council
stacks; towers overwritten with grey-green
shrubs, roughed up by blown cloud
and the fluid silt of pigeons fattened on
microwave rice.

We retreated, blinking into adolescence;
rooms plied with TV and cheap booze, afraid
now of anything that could parrot the stinging
softness of another's careful touch.

Their city is a mound that quakes, dense nest
locked in a copse of narrow rowans.
They walk there still.
Ageless. Without burden.

Nocturnal Toolbox

Let them perish, those who have uttered
our words before.

I stole that line from Samuel Beckett,
Who half-inched it himself from Saint Jerome,
Fenced on the way by Boswell's *Life of Johnson*,
A brutal crime committed by such an extraordinary tome.

I snuck in at night with no one looking,
And stuffed the scrap of language in a sack,
Piano wire and bolt cutters are the pride of any poet,
Raw elements of our covert spoliation.

So I climbed down the back stairs, absconded with the sentence
Suspended from my shoulder like the finest swag,
And now it hangs on the mantel of this poem,
Calling for the death of the one who dared to bring it home.

Covenant

for the Calder Valley

The river wells up with branches and dislodged scum,

an iron foam works its way across the valley

winding wildly, drunk on damage.

Tongues of contaminated mud

lick paper from the walls, gulping down books

and cabinets and TV stands.

Fuses close their eyes at once, all resistance gone.

The council point to lack of funds, patting

their fat pockets like charades, all the time

the hills keep burning, empty of trees, dead

of wood. A thousand miles away

the Prime Minister fucks his seventh wife, poorly

and without love. The split and crackle of moor flames

spread the news across the county:

disappointment always follows fire,

follows flood. Thunderheads swallow

three more weeks of sky, promising

further rain, whilst downstream two deer wash up

on the tarmac slab of a motorway

service station, eyes bulging, grunts drowned:

the inhabitants of some sick ark, a confused

vessel returning its covenant to the road.

Change of Knowledge

Mary, some days
you only come here to open my heart

to death, to show how one February
frost might corrode an old world just as a finger

snaps against a thumb. Your white crown
always an inscription of the soil

each slow grace of your hands an indulgence
withdrawn like a gift grief keeps on giving.

It was on a cold hill where a black church
stood beside another

the stone ruined by two long centuries
of smoke. Lung cancer, spread, just gone

seventy-six. The earth turned down
to a deep bed

laid over with rope and rough cloth.
School uniform the one smart thing

I could muster, worn sky, dressed in winter
cliché: grey clouds roaming

grey over grey, the white sun hollowing
a silverish decline.

The priest tried to teach me to trust
all unspeakable things to God

while I was lost in the descent
of roses, soaked through by dull prayers of mud,

the coffin lending you a weight
you never could have carried on your own.

Today the winter drips and sags
through its barren music,

the toneless sky and slop
of scum running in the ditches

clogged with these tissues of meaning,
the recrudescence of a single day

left behind decades of dark wood,
of rain.

Winter Window

for Peter Huchel

Evening gone, lost in afternoon's gullet.
The torn pages of a sky, grey slopes
folding through mottled fog, frail air thickened
by a cowardly light. Farms spread their lamps
onto the meadow, blue ponds seethe with foam.
Tomorrow lies down low in the churchyard,
ice-scuffed branches separate dusk from dusk.

Pigeons clad the December eaves, ticks and feathers
smear Gethsemane's bough. The window leaks
its ancient colour, eyes glassy and harlequined
with lead. Dark leaves gather around a lone alder
blanketed by snow. Out among the reeling gulls
a tired bell rubs salt into the wind.

We turn away, draw the curtains
in the room, the cold world gone.
Bodies lost to one another's heat, hands and mouths
settled in the hollows, in the soft pressures we call home.
There in the sleep of shadowed cloth, the mark
of winter, rasped and burly at the throat,
shrivels into the smoothest ember of a voice.

Family Holiday

The house bore our name
but was never ours,
purchased by some
skeletal success story
some dry sort without the habit
for drink. We were *just visiting*—
haunting's poor relation, cases
stuffed with sun cream,
poppies, sandwich meat: a picture
postcard of Renault overspill.

Waking to the white ache
of a sunlit terrace, pink aniseed
in the glass, the slushed ice
of slurred speech. Aphasic
afternoons dipped
in the under-thrum,
the wing-clap of insect radio,
spark and scrape of old tin
nesting in the fruit trees.

Sunburnt hands shaking sugar cube
dice, three kings and two nines swimming
in blue-green heat, crystal
light blistered on our backs,
days left lost among pines,
the pale stones looking out to sea:
smooth hopes wishing with us,
trying so hard to be gone.

An Imagined Visit to the Pencil Museum

As you've probably guessed
I've never been, but this is not the time

to quibble with existence. I'd arrive
the night before of course,

driving northward in the dusklight,
and check-in to my top-notch B&B

chosen for its five star rating
antique features

and several comments stressing both
comfort and dear repose.

The next day I'd stroll beneath the pencil
pines, admiring their grey needles

and the fluted shavings they use
instead of leaves.

Next I'd scuttle through the graphite
mine, the soft caves of smudge and glint,

where I could write my name in stalactites
and touch the weeping walls

feeling my skin erase
the thinnest surface of the dark.

After, they'd show me the pencils
carved from moonlight

and those extinct reptiles
whose teeth can serve as glue.

Last of all I'd do the gift shop,
shedding my gold coins with aplomb:

half a kilo of liquorice
crayons, twelve kinds of mechanical lead,

even Paul the three-foot talking pencil,
who whimpers *hold me* when you squeeze his hand,

and the resin statue, a small facsimile,
from the last great sharpening tournament

of 1992. In the car I'd be
exhausted, scuffed wild in carbonic joy,

Paul and I would have fun talking
with sunlight cross-hatching through the cloud.

We'd stay there late watching the sky edge down
to a blue plumbago,

shade chewing the corners where the car park
met the wood, both fearful of the drive before us

along the darkened windings of the road
and back into the nowhere I began.

Haw

Laugh twice
at the false aristocracy

whose fascist propaganda keeps
your teeth gritted
       set hard against its mother tongue.

Britain calling, Britain calling
the airwaves lit by red crosses

parading their centuries of damage
between these barren amusements of coast.

Keep smiling;
walk on the pavilion lawn in moonlight
       abandon yourself to language

and call the rain-soaked earth
a fiction one more time.

Familiar Road

Icy evening. Drunk but not too drunk.
A blur of lights round Hollingworth, where blue
unhappy boats skim the winter lake.
Your breath gleams up the window of your
clapped-out Volvo estate, the dark red hulk,
that snug vessel which covered our childhood
miles, expanses doled out in weekend tropes:
car-boot sales, bacon-sausage-egg, tea scalding through
Styrofoam, and fish fried in brown batter.
The coruscating iron of time well spent.
Twice round the clock before it got to us,
journeys already written, the dashboard
lit up by other lives carried in long numbers.

One gin, three whiskeys, and the rest,
a spray of snow irks you with a skid and
now suddenly you're liquid—all surface and give.
It's too late for me to whisper *drive slow*—
mercurial, wax-winged you slip
in mixed myth, leafless crack of black branches,
split of frost-spun twigs. Even now the correctness
of their frailty is not wasted on you.
Dark red and unkempt you slap down deep in
the Calder, bothersome sirens whirr
with distance, blue unhappy sounds
demanding explanation. The wet scarp
sludged with wheel ruts, what luck, to find
yourself in these unlikely waters: cracked, fractured,
wounded and water-logged. On reflection
there's blood, coins, and a broken mobile phone:
your pockets tell you that you'll be out late.

Stuck amid the mud, the creeping
maroon, you feel relief, the lost weight
of not having to go one single mile more.

Apophatic

The birth of the world. A ruined sign
expanding.

A black sun extends coiled withdrawals
of cypress.

Pomegranates: foetid, sour,
succoured by flies.

Speech is a museum, the word a tank
for perfumed fish: frilled, irrelevant.

Fruit softens into wakening,
our mouths re-grown in silent moistures.

The morning is a glance, neither
eternity nor time.

White blossom crowds a winter tree.
Earth's reassertion: a tectonic shift.

I retreat into your thickening dark
committing blasphemies
common to hand and tongue.

To devour is a prayer:
the cannibal
repudiates loss beyond all measure.

Robert Mitchum

a storm is blowing in from Paradise
Walter Benjamin

Backward angel, carrying a love/hate mouth

to match the hands, pumping gas on highway asphalt,

your tarry brawn pushing my tongue

around North American language. Diner cheeks,

eyes at sunset, chin half-cut: a sickle

carving out two faces both turned away

from good. Smoke drifting over lowered lids

too tranquil for the sting of rhythm,

every shot a drawl, a question, framed as if

to say *what next?* History's a mug's game:

making moves behind our backs,

but one you'll play again for a chance to get clean

of these dead sentences, words and voices

that haunt the canyon, wheels spinning

back to catastrophe, all those spectres

blowing silver through the pines.

First Anniversary
for J.

A foolish lunge to Hastings for a Jacuzzi
bath and a Japanese toilet equipped

with built-in radio, our bedsit B&B
a half-converted love hotel:

all mirrored ceilings, palm tree murals and three kinds
of granola, asbestos thick and chewy as drywall.

Flushed pink and drunk on bubbles we squatted
in the outdoor pool, ankle-deep and under-lit,

crowded with *froufrou* ferns, the atmosphere
seedy and oxygenated: a plump swamp.

A couple in matching swimwear sidled crabwise
along the shallow pit, eyes secreting

indecent proposals, a whiff of gin
and car keys. We scuttled out in seconds,

back to safe sex and unbranded Cava, hot tub frolics
and long kisses as the toilet hummed out its doleful tune.

We woke blurred and naked to heavy cloud
and broad winds, painted palms now hurricane

portents, bath bubbles a warning of storm waters.
On the seafront we slugged hot chips, blistered

and scraped by pebble rain, scarred sideways, heads
ducking in and out of amusements, hands gripped tight

hoping to weather the thunder, buffed around by
choppy plumes of lightning. On the walk back we met

a grey gull dragging abandoned bags: roast chicken,
Brillo pads and two imported lagers

hooped beneath its blood-tipped beak. Together
we plunged into traffic, cheering him on,

screeching and car horns mixed with laughter, dust
kicked up in a swirl of crisp packets and dry leaves,

caught in a brutish churn of motion, glad for
someone else to be sharing our good time.

Duration

Sun-yard bearing a cold north light,
yellow jasmine scuffs the fences,
magnolias open on the long road,
old blossoms like white sands giving their
fine bodies to the wind.
We record this clumsy botany, infected
by the grammar of spring, our hearts taken
by the earth's blunt fecundity,
the rooted smell of mulch and fox leavings
feeding the soil its temptation to move on.

From the window I watch
starlings peck and sway through timber,
nesting in next door's roof-edge, wings flitting,
speckled bodies ripping twigs and fig leaves
to furnish their soft corner of the void.
On the lawn below children run and scream,
their bodies quick to trust the day's new heat
and the bright water as it gurgles from the hose,
feet bare on the mown grass
blind with the joy of forces in motion.

Getting Over It

i.m. Oliver Bernard

A third decade walks in carrying back
Pain and an unreasonable desire
For health—a big ask after the roaring
Disporting twenties, those long nights drugged and
Dragged across the lavender miles of dawn.

Now the nights come home early, brandishing
Loose smiles and comfortably drunk; bedded
Pleasures promising a kind of daylight
Saving before the morning's comedy, that lewd
Troupe of slight aches rehearsing in the muscle.

The kitchen basks in an apophatics
Of unknown tasks, the blank stares of pepper
Pots, olive oil, and flaked salt cruel as frost
Sharp-edging winter light. The gas ring mumbles
Blue fire: answers burnt sore at the tip of tongues.

Sudden comes a taste for simple rhythm,
A spade, cloven earth, a seed row driven.
My voice grows thick, quarrying weight from the
Gravel of remembered smoke, soot given
Sureness by a capacity for giving up.

In the far sky a dim spot glooms
Horizon cloud, the eye narrows toward
New shadow—a darkness not close but there.

Shell

Calcified light-splitter, dirt sifter, I hold you,
bruise of petrol picked from the rough shore, tithe
levied by waves, a tender token of
land-sea exchange. My surf spoil,
I turn you, loose eyelid
grazed by our cold covenant of moon rock.
I know you, drifter:
the very definition of coast.

The hand, the ear, one draws up the other,
vaulted by the promise of an echo,
the hand comes now,
comes to the ear, scaly shuck of rainbow
pressed against this carbon copy, sinew
wired for sound. Hear! A murmur comes rising
through the furrowed cup, whorl-playing,
fingering the drumskin, cave of pressure
and bones, our blood surges
and in your name we call it *ocean*.

Hebden Bridge

Wool skies turn over heavy cloud,
the pages of a good book stuck somewhere
between wickedness and flood. A gurgle
of rain meadows, pitches unfit for sport,
long hedgerows littered with chap-sticks, cider
bottles, and damp tubes of old fireworks:
their excitements decidedly past tense.

This is the place you still call *home*,
an answer arrived at just by asking
the wrong question too many times.
The landscape an impossible pattern of fields,
drystone and cart tracks, brickwork lines
tangled around dark farms,
terraces milled in childish strokes
of grit; raw-edged and smoky.

The canal churns through creaking locks,
bleak with weed and fat perch and reeds,
where shadows of imported carp
nudge blunt snouts through the thickened silt.
Men sit switching stories on damp canvas,
stools sunk low in the towpath,
one hand on a sandwich, another dipped
in the red husks of maggots, the fresh bait
struggling free, fluffed like rice, writhing too.

Shop-fronts boarded or bought-up, shaken dry
and franchised into nowhere: chrome and steel,
exposed light-bulbs, railway salvage,
their high chairs polished by the acutest music.

You can still buy crystals, eye talismans,
and stone webs for catching dreams; false
promise as unorthodox practice, strung out
on silk. Commerce the one sure way to heal
the wounds time has forced you into keeping.

Fifteen pubs. Three per thousand. More yesterday.
Rooms where you can watch the same face age
through its endless afternoons.
Doorways hung with pretty chimes, wicker
and knotted twigs, scents of incense,
marks of incest, park benches warped
in a fug of weed and needles.
Out beyond the council blocks lie
the sewage plant and dump, broken dye-works
and coal silos; industrial leftovers clumped
with white goods and rust, jaws and iron arms
crushing waste, weary of reconstitution.

Hold on, there are still the old mills, oak woods,
and carpets of bluebells, millponds
still with sediment, and the great moors swept
hard like a birthplace for the wind.
The whole place picture perfect, yes a land
where poetry comes easy, skimming the dark crags
and fattened beeches growing high
above the river murk, voices cheering, drowning
out the yeasty spume and froth, brimming deep,
lower even than the world.

Notes

The epigraph is taken from Isaac Rosenberg's poem 'Expression' in *The Collected Poems of Isaac Rosenberg* (Chatto & Windus).

'Nocturnal Toolbox' – Background information for this poem was cribbed from *Samuel Beckett's Library* by Mark Nixon and Dirk Van Hulle.

'A Change of Knowledge' – This poem is in memory of my grandmother, Mary Wilson.

'Haw' – The word haw has a number of connotations to the natural world and to language, denoting both the fruit of the hawthorn and an intermission or hesitation in speech. Lord Haw-Haw was a name associated with William Joyce, a fascist and broadcaster of Nazi propaganda during the Second World War.

'Apophatic' – This poem is a product of the deep impression made by, in particular, two books: Denys Turner's *The Darkness of God* and Julia Kristeva's *Black Sun: Depression and Melancholia*.

'Robert Mitchum' – This poem is for Karen Solie.

Acknowledgements & Thanks

A cup of Yorkshire tea for the editors of the following publications where several of these poems first appeared, sometimes in slightly different form: *Acumen, Anthropocene Poetry, Black Bough Poetry, Burning House Press, New World Writing, The London Magazine, Wildfire Words*.

'Gospel Oak to Barking' was awarded third prize in *The London Magazine* 2019 Poetry Competition.

Thanks to: Martha Sprackland and Steven O'Brien for their encouragement and guidance; to Ben, with whom I wrote my first poems, aged 17 (usually about dead whales); Will, who submitted to more drunken live readings than anyone; to my folks for letting me grow up around books; and to Mark, my wonderful friend and guide without whom none of this would be possible.

Thanks to everyone at **ignition**press.

Finally, to Juno, my love, for everything.

MIX
Paper from responsible sources
FSC® C007326

Oxford Brookes is committed to the environment.
This document is printed using processes that are:

100% carbon positive | 100% EMAS | 100% renewable energy | 100% ISO14001 | 100% eco-friendly simitri® toner | 100% recycled FSC® stock | Zero 0% waste to landfill

Printed by **seacourt** – proud to be counted amongst the top environmental printers in the world